W9-BKG-298

THE BATTLE OF
GUADALCANAL

LAND AND SEA WARFARE
IN THE SOUTH PACIFIC

By **Larry Hama** Illustrated by **Anthony Williams**

Rosen Classroom Books & Materials™
New York

Published in 2007 by The Rosen Publishing Group, Inc.
29 East 21st Street, New York, NY 10010

First edition, 2007

Simone Drinkwater, Series Editor, Osprey Publishing
Nel Yomtov, Series Editor, Rosen Book Works

Library of Congress Cataloging-in-Publication Data

Hama, Larry.
  The battle of Guadalcanal : land and sea warfare in the South Pacific / by
  Larry Hama. — 1st ed.
  p. cm. — (Graphic battles of World War II)
  Includes index.
  ISBN-13   978-1-4042-0784-4 (lib.)   978-1-4042-7426-6 (pbk.)
  ISBN-10   1-4042-0784-8 (lib.)   1-4042-7426-X (pbk.)
  6-pack ISBN-13   978-1-4042-7427-3   6-pack ISBN-10   1-4042-7427-8

  1. Guadalcanal, Battle of, Solomon Islands, 1942–1943–Juvenile literature. I. Title.
  II. Series

  D767.98.H265 2007
  940.54'265933–dc22

                                        2006037336

Manufactured in the United States of America

CPSIA Compliance Information: Batch #WR111310RC:
For Further Information contact Rosen Publishing, New York, New York at 1-800-237-9932

CONTENTS

WORLD WAR II, 1939-1945

At the time Japan attacked the U.S. naval base at Pearl Harbor in December 1941, war was waging in several parts of the world. Germany and Italy were battling many of their European neighbors, and Japan was fighting nations in Asia.

The Japanese plan of battle was to extend their control in the Pacific Ocean region. Right after their successful attack on Pearl Harbor, Japan aggressively took control of numerous territories in the Pacific. Finally, in May and June 1942, the Americans and their allies defeated the Japanese in the battles of the Coral Sea and Midway. These victories at last gave the Allies a chance to launch a strong offensive to stop Japanese expansion.

Guadalcanal was to be one of the key battle sites. Fighting on the small island began in August 1942 and lasted for six months. The struggle included land battles, naval battles, and daily aircraft battles. Often referred to as the "turning point" of the war, Guadalcanal marked the change in power in the Pacific region.

KEY COMMANDERS

Vice Admiral William F. Halsey Jr.
Commanded the U.S. Third Fleet in the Pacific against Japan. His slogan, "Hit hard, hit fast, hit often," earned him the nickname "Bull."

Major General Alexander A. Vandegrift
Commander of the 1st Marine Division, he had previously served in many of America's battles in South America and China. His actions on Guadalcanal earned him the Medal of Honor.

Lieutenant General Harukichi Hyakutake
Commander of the Japanese 17th Army, he led the Guadalcanal campaign. He underestimated his foe and sent too few troops into battle.

Lieutenant General Masao Maruyama
An experienced commander who had beaten Allied forces earlier, he believed that the Japanese Bushido (fighting spirit) could conquer all of his nation's enemies.

On May 3, 1942, Japanese forces occupied the Pacific islands of Guadalcanal and Tulagi. This was part of their campaign to capture New Guinea and isolate America's allies, Australia and New Zealand. The Allies made plans to recapture the two small islands.

At this time, most of America's fighting resources were being used in Europe against Germany and Italy. American war production was still in its early stages. Many types of supplies were scarce in the Pacific war against the Japanese. Also, Allied losses had been high in the Pacific, with the Japanese winning battle after battle.

Henderson Field on Guadalcanal was an important airfield for both Americans and Japanese. Once Americans took control of the airfield, Japanese planes were at risk of being attacked when flying near the island.

Nevertheless, on August 7, 1942, U.S. Marines landed at Tulagi and Guadalcanal, supported by what remained of the U.S. and Australian fleets. On the night of August 9, Japanese cruisers sank three American cruisers and one Australian cruiser in a battle off Savo Island. The Japanese ignored the Allied transports and supply ships, and the helpless vessels fled the next day. The 15,000 marines on Guadalcanal were on their own.

On August 13, the Americans took control of the airfield on Guadalcanal, naming it Henderson Field. Japanese ships could no longer approach Guadalcanal by day, because American planes flying from Henderson would bomb them.

Also, Japanese ships could not count on air support from their carriers because the Japanese carrier fleet had been destroyed at the Battle of Midway in June.

However, the Japanese navy was able to reach Guadalcanal at nighttime. By day, American ships would arrive and unload men and supplies, and then leave. At night, Japanese warships would come to the island, land troops, shell the marines, and then withdraw before dawn.

On the night of August 20, Colonel Kiyono Ichiki attacked the Americans across the Tenaru River. He and most of his men were killed in the fighting. About 3,000 Japanese

The Japanese destroyer *Kikutsuki* was one of the ships that participated in the invasion of Tulagi on May 3, 1942. The next day it was bombed and sunk in an air raid by the United States.

reinforcements under General Kiyotaki Kawaguchi were sent to the island. The first attempt to land them was defeated at sea on August 24. Kawaguchi's troops had to land by night at Taivu Point.

One week later, a U.S. Marine Raider battalion attacked Kawaguchi's base. They wrecked his artillery, destroyed supplies and reserve ammunition, and took away maps, documents, and even the trousers of Kawaguchi's dress uniform!

On the night of September 12, the Kawaguchi Brigade attacked the marine Raider battalion. Initially pushed back, the marines managed to hold a second time. The next night, Kawaguchi again attacked, but he failed to break through and lost a third of his force.

However, despite their success against Kawaguchi's powerful assaults, not everything was going well for the Americans.

This U.S. Marine tank and its crew were part of the force that defeated Colonel Ichiki and his men at the Tenaru River.

On August 31, the U.S. carrier *Saratoga* was torpedoed by Japanese submarine *I-26*. On September 15, six torpedoes from submarine *I-19* sank the carrier *Wasp* and a destroyer and knocked the battleship *North Carolina* out of the Guadalcanal fight.

But the Japanese were having their problems, too. After the destruction of Kawaguchi's Brigade, the Japanese army realized it would have to send two new divisions to Guadalcanal, both under the command of Lt. General Masao Maruyama. Reinforcements would be sent to Guadalcanal in convoys, little by little.

The Americans called these

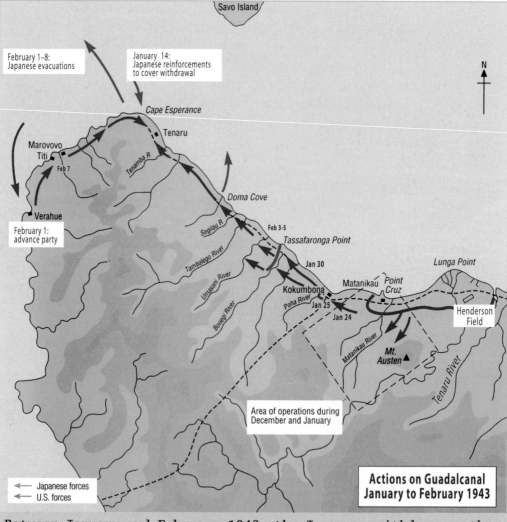

February 1–8:
Japanese evacuations

January 14:
Japanese reinforcements
to cover withdrawal

Savo Island

N

Cape Esperance

Tenaru

Marovovo
Titi

Feb 7

Tenamiba R.

Doma Cove

Verahue

February 1:
advance party

Segilau R.

Feb 3-5

Tassafaronga Point

Tambalego River

Umasani River

Jan 30

Lunga Point

Kokumbona

Matanikau

Point
Cruz

Bonegi River

Poha River

Jan 25

Jan 24

Henderson
Field

Matanikau River

Mt.
Austen

Tenaru River

Area of operations during
December and January

Japanese forces
U.S. forces

**Actions on Guadalcanal
January to February 1943**

Between January and February 1943, the Japanese withdrew, rather than lose more men in a fight they knew they had lost. They sent a small number of reinforcements as a distraction, while preparing the rest of their troops for evacuation.

Japanese general Tadashi Sumiyama attacked U.S. Marines with tanks and infantry on the west side of Guadalcanal. The attack failed. This photo shows a destroyed Japanese tank as it sinks into the sand.

convoys the Tokyo Express. On the night of October 11, U.S. admiral Norman Scott ambushed a convoy, sinking a cruiser and a destroyer. At dawn, planes from Henderson got two more destroyers. But the Japanese troops were still landed with heavy artillery.

The Japanese began shelling U.S. forces. On October 13, a Japanese task force knocked out the main airfield. The next day, Japanese bombers attacked. On October 15, U.S. planes attacked Japanese transports unloading in daylight. They sank three. The others fled. The Japanese lost troops, supplies, and Maruyama's artillery ammunition.

Maruyama pressed on. He hoped to launch a major attack on the airfield. It was to be supported by air and naval gunfire and what remained of Kawaguchi and Ichiki's troops to the east. Poor intelligence, poor communications, rain, and the jungle terrain turned the attack into a series of uncoordinated blows.

First to attack was General Tadashi Sumiyama on October 23. He attacked the western perimeter along the coast. Marine artillery knocked out his tanks and destroyed his infantry. Maruyama's main attack was made in two separate parts from the south. Many of his men were sick, starving, and exhausted. His often-postponed attack began on October 24 and failed miserably.

The Americans had just appointed a new commander for the Guadalcanal campaign, William "Bull" Halsey. On October 25, Japanese battleships again bombarded the marines. The day after that, Halsey was told that a large Japanese fleet was approaching. He sent a three-word order to his carriers:

"ATTACK REPEAT ATTACK."

The October 26 Battle of Santa Cruz saw the loss of the U.S. carrier *Hornet* and severe damage to the carrier *Enterprise*. Of the four Japanese carriers, two were damaged, but all withdrew. The Americans still held Guadalcanal and Henderson Field. With its defeat at Guadalcanal, Japan was forced to fight a defensive war, leading to many critical Allied victories in the Pacific.

THE BATTLE OF GUADALCANAL
LAND AND SEA WARFARE IN THE SOUTH PACIFIC

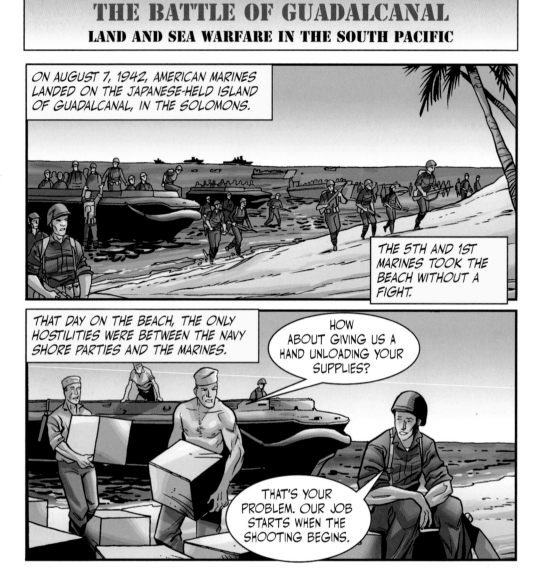

ON AUGUST 7, 1942, AMERICAN MARINES LANDED ON THE JAPANESE-HELD ISLAND OF GUADALCANAL, IN THE SOLOMONS.

THE 5TH AND 1ST MARINES TOOK THE BEACH WITHOUT A FIGHT.

THAT DAY ON THE BEACH, THE ONLY HOSTILITIES WERE BETWEEN THE NAVY SHORE PARTIES AND THE MARINES.

HOW ABOUT GIVING US A HAND UNLOADING YOUR SUPPLIES?

THAT'S YOUR PROBLEM. OUR JOB STARTS WHEN THE SHOOTING BEGINS.

BUT THE QUESTION OF SUPPLIES WAS EVERYBODY'S PROBLEM.

BOTH THE JAPANESE AND THE AMERICAN FORCES FOUGHT THE CAMPAIGN OF GUADALCANAL AT THE FARTHEST LIMIT OF THEIR SUPPLY LINES.

TOKYO

SAN FRANCISCO 5,000

PACIFIC OCEAN

TOKYO 3,600

HONOLULU 3,300

PAPUA NEW GUINEA

GUADALCANAL

NOT TO SCALE

THE JAPANESE FORCES ON GUADALCANAL WERE SUPPLIED FROM RABAUL, PAPUA NEW GUINEA. THEIR SHIPS HAD TO PASS THROUGH A CHANNEL BETWEEN THE ISLANDS IN THE SOLOMON CHAIN.

TO RABAUL

THE SLOT

THAT CHANNEL WAS CALLED "THE SLOT."

GUADALCANAL

9

VICE ADMIRAL ROBERT L. GHORMLEY WAS IN OVERALL COMMAND OF THE AMERICAN FORCES IN THE SOUTH PACIFIC.

HE MAY HAVE BEEN A GOOD LEADER AND PLANNER, BUT HE NEVER WENT TO GUADALCANAL TO SEE THE SITUATION FIRSTHAND.

VICE ADMIRAL FRANK J. FLETCHER WAS IN CHARGE OF THE NAVAL FLEET TASK FORCE FOR THE INVASION OF GUADALCANAL.

HAVING LOST AN AIRCRAFT CARRIER AT THE BATTLE OF THE CORAL SEA AND ANOTHER AT MIDWAY, FLETCHER WAS DANGEROUSLY OVERCAUTIOUS.

REAR ADMIRAL RICHMOND K. TURNER COMMANDED THE AMPHIBIOUS* FORCES AT GUADALCANAL. HE WAS A TACTICAL GENIUS...

...BUT HE DIDN'T GET ALONG WELL WITH GENERAL ALEXANDER A. VANDEGRIFT WHO LED THE LANDING FORCE.

*FORCES THAT ARE TRANSPORTED BY VEHICLES SUCH AS LANDING CRAFT, WHICH WORK ON LAND AND SEA, AND ATTACK UPON LANDING.

AS SUPPLIES PILED UP ON THE NARROW BEACH, THE MARINES PUSHED INLAND.

THE JAPANESE HAD ALMOST COMPLETED AN AIRFIELD ON THE NORTHERN PLAIN OF GUADALCANAL.

THAT WAS TOO EASY.

AFTER A BRIEF FIGHT, THE MARINES TOOK THE AIR-FIELD AND RENAMED IT HENDERSON FIELD.

IT WAS EASY BECAUSE THE JAPANESE COMMAND HAD ORDERED THEIR TROOPS IN THE AREA TO HIDE IN THE HILLS UNTIL THE AMERICANS LEFT.

THEY THOUGHT WHAT WAS HAPPENING WAS ONLY A RAID, NOT AN INVASION.

11

ADMIRAL FLETCHER, CONCERNED ABOUT LOSSES AND LACK OF FUEL, DECIDED TO WITHDRAW HIS AIRCRAFT CARRIER GROUP FROM THE AREA.

WITHOUT AIR COVER, THE AMPHIBIOUS FLEET WAS LEFT UNPROTECTED, SO ADMIRAL TURNER OPTED FOR THEIR WITHDRAWAL AS WELL.

THIS WOULD HAVE LEFT VANDEGRIFT'S MARINES STRANDED ON GUADALCANAL WITH ONLY HALF THEIR SUPPLIES AND NO AIR SUPPORT.

VANDEGRIFT COMPLAINED BITTERLY. THE FLEETS LEFT ANYWAY.

MEANWHILE, A JAPANESE FLEET WAS APPROACHING THE AMERICAN CRUISERS AND DESTROYERS THAT REMAINED ON SCREENING DUTY.

THOSE ARE JAPANESE SCOUT PLANES, SIR!

FLYING WITH RECOGNITION LIGHTS ON? THEY HAVE TO BE OURS!

THEY WEREN'T.

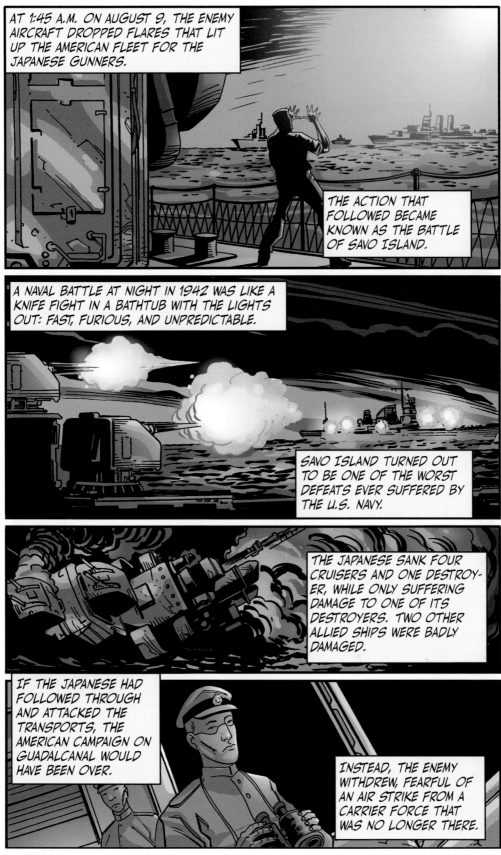

AT 1:45 A.M. ON AUGUST 9, THE ENEMY AIRCRAFT DROPPED FLARES THAT LIT UP THE AMERICAN FLEET FOR THE JAPANESE GUNNERS.

THE ACTION THAT FOLLOWED BECAME KNOWN AS THE BATTLE OF SAVO ISLAND.

A NAVAL BATTLE AT NIGHT IN 1942 WAS LIKE A KNIFE FIGHT IN A BATHTUB WITH THE LIGHTS OUT: FAST, FURIOUS, AND UNPREDICTABLE.

SAVO ISLAND TURNED OUT TO BE ONE OF THE WORST DEFEATS EVER SUFFERED BY THE U.S. NAVY.

THE JAPANESE SANK FOUR CRUISERS AND ONE DESTROYER, WHILE ONLY SUFFERING DAMAGE TO ONE OF ITS DESTROYERS. TWO OTHER ALLIED SHIPS WERE BADLY DAMAGED.

IF THE JAPANESE HAD FOLLOWED THROUGH AND ATTACKED THE TRANSPORTS, THE AMERICAN CAMPAIGN ON GUADALCANAL WOULD HAVE BEEN OVER.

INSTEAD, THE ENEMY WITHDREW, FEARFUL OF AN AIR STRIKE FROM A CARRIER FORCE THAT WAS NO LONGER THERE.

13

THE JAPANESE 17TH ARMY UNDER THE COMMAND OF GENERAL HARUKICHI HYAKUTAKE WAS ORDERED TO RETAKE GUADALCANAL.

THE FIRST OF A SERIES OF CONVOYS THAT WERE TO BECOME KNOWN AS THE "TOKYO EXPRESS" DELIVERED THE INITIAL ASSAULT UNITS LED BY COLONEL KIYONO ICHIKI.

ICHIKI WAS UNDER THE MISTAKEN IMPRESSION THAT A SMALL RAIDING PARTY OF MARINES WAS ALL THAT WAS HOLDING THE AIRFIELD.

ON THE WAY, THEY CAPTURED SGT. JACOB VOUZA OF THE NATIVE POLICE. VOUZA HAD RETIRED IN 1941 AFTER 25 YEARS OF SERVICE.

HE MARCHED HIS TROOPS TOWARD HENDERSON FIELD.

HE RETURNED TO DUTY WORKING FOR THE BRITISH FORCES AFTER THE JAPANESE INVADED HIS HOME ISLAND. HE HAD BEEN SCOUTING FOR THE AMERICANS WHEN HE WAS CAUGHT.

VOUZA WAS TORTURED AND QUESTIONED FOR HOURS, BUT REFUSED TO BETRAY THE AMERICANS.

AFTER BEING BAYONETED, HE WAS LEFT FOR DEAD.

BUT VOUZA FOUGHT ON AND RACED THROUGH THE JUNGLE AHEAD OF THE JAPANESE COLUMN...

...TO WARN THE MARINES WHO WERE DUG IN AT THE MOUTH OF WHAT WAS THEN THOUGHT TO BE THE TENARU RIVER.

THE MARINES WERE READY WHEN ICHIKI'S FORCES ATTACKED.

IT IS BELIEVED THAT COLONEL ICHIKI WAS KILLED LEADING ONE OF THE CHARGES.

WHEN NIGHT FELL, THE BATTLE OF THE TENARU WAS STILL RAGING.

PRIVATE ALBERT SCHMID AND CORPORAL LEROY DIAMOND WERE NOT GOING TO LET THE ENEMY PASS.

A JAPANESE GRENADE BLINDED SCHMID.

DIAMOND, WOUNDED EARLIER, WAS INCAPABLE OF FIRING THE MACHINE GUN.

NONE OF THIS WAS ENOUGH TO STOP TWO DETERMINED MARINES.

WHERE ARE THEY, LEE?

SHOOT TO THE LEFT, SMITTY!*

*LEE AND SMITTY WERE DIAMOND AND SCHMID'S NICKNAMES FOR EACH OTHER.

THE LINE HELD, AND ON THE MORNING OF AUGUST 21, THE MARINES COUNTERATTACKED AND DESTROYED THE REMAINDER OF ICHIKI'S ILL-PREPARED FORCES.

ON AUGUST 24, IN AN AIRCRAFT CARRIER DUEL CALLED THE BATTLE OF THE EASTERN SOLOMONS, JAPANESE LIGHT CARRIER *RYUJO* WAS SUNK...

...AND THE AMERICAN CARRIER *ENTERPRISE* WAS SEVERELY DAMAGED.

ONE WEEK LATER, JAPANESE SUBMARINE *I-26*, CAPTAINED BY MINORU YOKOTA, CAUGHT A U.S. CARRIER IN ITS SIGHTS.

SA-RA-TO-GA DESU!*

*IT'S THE *SARATOGA!*

THE *I-26* LAUNCHED A SIX-TORPEDO SALVO AT THE CARRIER, WHICH WAS 3,830 YARDS AWAY, AND MAKING 13 KNOTS.*

*ABOUT 15 MPH

ONLY ONE TORPEDO HIT THE *SARATOGA*, BUT IT WAS ENOUGH TO SEND THE SHIP BACK TO PEARL HARBOR FOR MAJOR REPAIRS.

THREE U.S. DESTROYERS REPORTED SINKING THE *I-26* WITH DEPTH CHARGES, BUT CAPTAIN YOKOTA HAD ALREADY SLIPPED AWAY.

17

IN EARLY SEPTEMBER, THE MARINES HEARD REPORTS FROM NATIVE SCOUTS THAT THOUSANDS OF JAPANESE WERE FORTIFYING THE VILLAGE OF TASIMBOKO.

MARINE INTELLIGENCE DID NOT BELIEVE IT, BUT IT WAS DECIDED TO SEND THE 1ST RAIDER BATTALION AND THE 1ST PARACHUTE BATTALION IN A COMBINED RAID.

THE RAIDING PARTY, LED BY COL. MERRITT A. EDSON, MET FIERCE AND ORGANIZED RESISTANCE.

THE JAPANESE FORCE, ESTIMATED AT NUMBERING 1,000, WERE WELL ARMED AND SUPPORTED BY FIELD ARTILLERY FIRING AT POINT-BLANK RANGE.

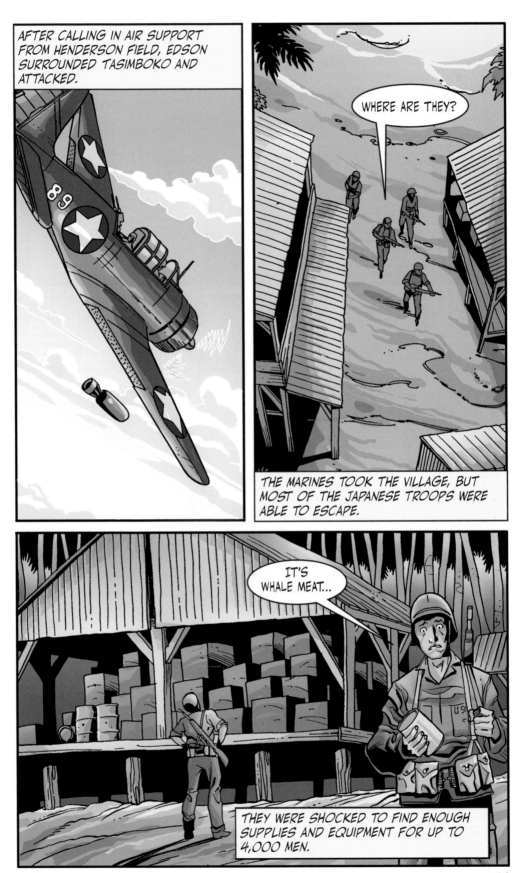

AFTER CALLING IN AIR SUPPORT FROM HENDERSON FIELD, EDSON SURROUNDED TASIMBOKO AND ATTACKED.

WHERE ARE THEY?

THE MARINES TOOK THE VILLAGE, BUT MOST OF THE JAPANESE TROOPS WERE ABLE TO ESCAPE.

IT'S WHALE MEAT...

THEY WERE SHOCKED TO FIND ENOUGH SUPPLIES AND EQUIPMENT FOR UP TO 4,000 MEN.

EDSON'S RAIDERS HAD CAUGHT THE REAR SECURITY FORCE OF THE JAPANESE 35TH REGIMENT COMMANDED BY MAJOR GENERAL KIYOTAKI KAWAGUCHI.

THE KAWAGUCHI BRIGADE, AS IT WAS CALLED, WAS SNEAKING AROUND TO ATTACK HENDERSON FIELD FROM THE SOUTH.

NONE OF THIS WAS KNOWN TO THE MARINE COMMAND, BUT NATIVE SCOUTS HAD REPORTED INCREASED JAPANESE ACTIVITY SOUTH OF THE AIRFIELD.

EDSON'S RAIDERS WERE MOVED INTO DEFENSIVE POSITIONS SOUTH OF HENDERSON FIELD.

ON THE NIGHT OF SEPTEMBER 12, JAPANESE WARSHIPS SHELLED THE DUG-IN MARINES FOR TWENTY MINUTES...

...BEFORE THE KAWAGUCHI BRIGADE BEGAN A SERIES OF HUMAN WAVE ASSAULTS.

FACED WITH SUPERIOR NUMBERS, THE MARINES WITHDREW NORTHWARD AND ESTABLISHED A TIGHTER DEFENSIVE LINE.

THE MARINES DUG IN ACROSS A GEOGRAPHICAL FEATURE THAT WAS TO BECOME KNOWN AS THE "BLOODY RIDGE."

THE NEXT DAY, JAPANESE PLANES BOMBED THE RIDGE AS THE MARINES TRIED TO STRENGTHEN THEIR POSITIONS.

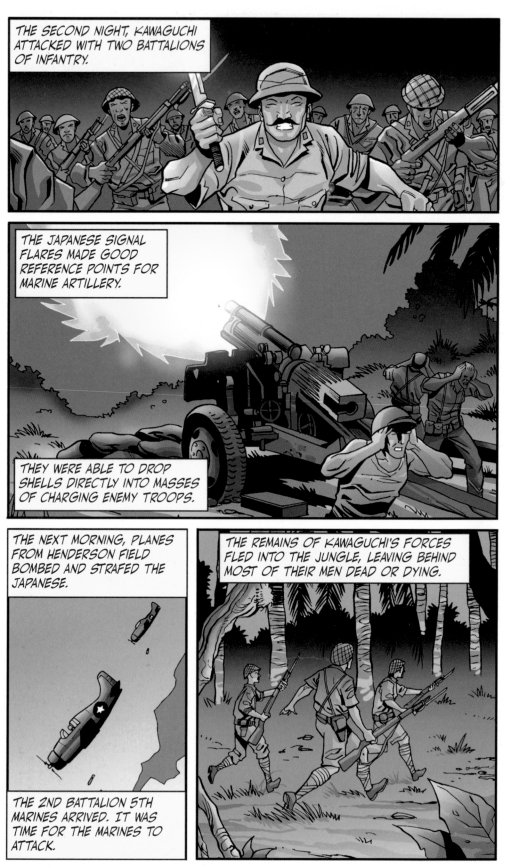

THE SECOND NIGHT, KAWAGUCHI ATTACKED WITH TWO BATTALIONS OF INFANTRY.

THE JAPANESE SIGNAL FLARES MADE GOOD REFERENCE POINTS FOR MARINE ARTILLERY.

THEY WERE ABLE TO DROP SHELLS DIRECTLY INTO MASSES OF CHARGING ENEMY TROOPS.

THE NEXT MORNING, PLANES FROM HENDERSON FIELD BOMBED AND STRAFED THE JAPANESE.

THE REMAINS OF KAWAGUCHI'S FORCES FLED INTO THE JUNGLE, LEAVING BEHIND MOST OF THEIR MEN DEAD OR DYING.

THE 2ND BATTALION 5TH MARINES ARRIVED. IT WAS TIME FOR THE MARINES TO ATTACK.

GENERAL HYAKUTAKE DRAFTED THE PLANS FOR THE OCTOBER JAPANESE OFFENSIVE TO TAKE BACK GUADALCANAL.

THEY WERE ELABORATE BATTLE PLANS, AND THE GENERAL WAS DISTRACTED AND DID NOT PRESS THE ADVANTAGE WHEN HE HAD IT.

ON OCTOBER 13, 1942, THE JAPANESE UNLEASHED A 24-BOMBER RAID ON HENDERSON FIELD.

THE AIRSTRIP WAS SO BADLY DAMAGED IT COULD ONLY BE USED FOR EMERGENCY LANDINGS.

JAPANESE HEAVY ARTILLERY, HIDDEN BEYOND THE RANGE OF MARINE ARTILLERY, POUNDED THE FIELD MERCILESSLY.

THE MARINES HAD A NAME FOR THE BIG GUNS: PISTOL PETE.

JAPANESE HEAVY CRUISERS BOMBARDED HENDERSON FIELD WITH THEIR 14-INCH GUNS.

EACH 14-INCH SHELL WEIGHED 1,400 POUNDS. THE BLAST THEY CREATED WHEN THEY HIT WAS ENORMOUS.

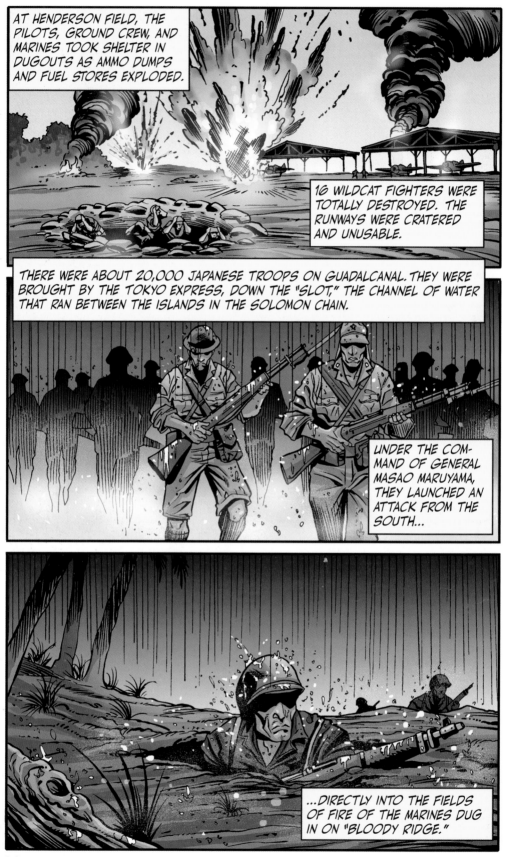

AT HENDERSON FIELD, THE PILOTS, GROUND CREW, AND MARINES TOOK SHELTER IN DUGOUTS AS AMMO DUMPS AND FUEL STORES EXPLODED.

16 WILDCAT FIGHTERS WERE TOTALLY DESTROYED. THE RUNWAYS WERE CRATERED AND UNUSABLE.

THERE WERE ABOUT 20,000 JAPANESE TROOPS ON GUADALCANAL. THEY WERE BROUGHT BY THE TOKYO EXPRESS, DOWN THE "SLOT," THE CHANNEL OF WATER THAT RAN BETWEEN THE ISLANDS IN THE SOLOMON CHAIN.

UNDER THE COMMAND OF GENERAL MASAO MARUYAMA, THEY LAUNCHED AN ATTACK FROM THE SOUTH...

...DIRECTLY INTO THE FIELDS OF FIRE OF THE MARINES DUG IN ON "BLOODY RIDGE."

COMMANDING ONE OF THE MARINE MACHINE GUN SECTIONS ON THE RIDGE WAS SGT. "MANILA JOHN" BASILONE.

WHEN ONE OF THE GUNS IN HIS SECTION WAS OVERRUN, BASILONE RAN TO PLUG THE GAP CARRYING A 41-LB. M1917 MACHINE GUN.

HE SURPRISED AND KILLED EIGHT ENEMY SOLDIERS. NO OTHER JAPANESE TROOPS GOT PAST HIM.

SGT. BASILONE MADE REPEATED RUNS TO GET MORE AMMO, ARMED ONLY WITH A PISTOL AND A MACHETE.

HE WAS OFFICIALLY CREDITED WITH KILLING 38 ENEMY SOLDIERS, BUT MORE THAN A THOUSAND DEAD WERE FOUND WITHIN THE SWEEP OF HIS GUNS.*

*ALTHOUGH MANY OF THESE CASUALTIES WERE PROBABLY CAUSED BY ARTILLERY.

THE MARINES HELD THE LINE ALL ALONG THE BLOODY RIDGE.

SEMPER FI!*

YOU SAID IT, BUDDY!

*SEMPER FIDELIS, OR ALWAYS FAITHFUL, THE MARINE MOTTO.

MARINE TANKS HAD TO SPRAY EACH OTHER WITH MACHINE GUN FIRE TO KEEP BAYONETS FROM BEING THRUST THROUGH THE VIEW-SLITS...

...AND GRENADES FROM BEING DROPPED DOWN THEIR HATCHES.

THE OUTLOOK WAS SO BAD THAT GENERAL VANDEGRIFT ORDERED A SECRET WITHDRAWAL PLAN TO BE DRAFTED.

LT. COL. MERRILL TWINING WROTE UP THE PLAN, BUT IT WAS NEVER USED.

WHEN GENERAL MARUYAMA CALLED OFF THE ATTACK, 1,500 OF HIS SOLDIERS WERE DEAD.

ALTHOUGH HENDERSON FIELD WAS KNOCKED OUT, AIR OPERATIONS CONTINUED FROM A SMALL STRIP A MILE TO THE EAST, CALLED "FIGHTER ONE."

THE PILOTS WHO FLEW OUT OF HENDERSON FIELD AND FIGHTER ONE CALLED THEMSELVES THE "CACTUS AIR FORCE."

AMONG THE CACTUS AIR FORCE PILOTS WAS CAPTAIN JOE FOSS, A RESERVIST FROM SOUTH DAKOTA.

ON ONE DAY OF FIERCE DOG-FIGHTING, OCTOBER 25TH, THE CACTUS AIR FORCE SHOT DOWN 22 JAPANESE PLANES.

CAPTAIN JOE FOSS ACCOUNTED FOR FOUR OF THEM.

DURING THE GUADALCANAL CAMPAIGN, JOE FOSS SHOT DOWN 26 ENEMY AIRCRAFT. HE WAS AWARDED THE CONGRESSIONAL MEDAL OF HONOR FOR HIS BRAVERY.

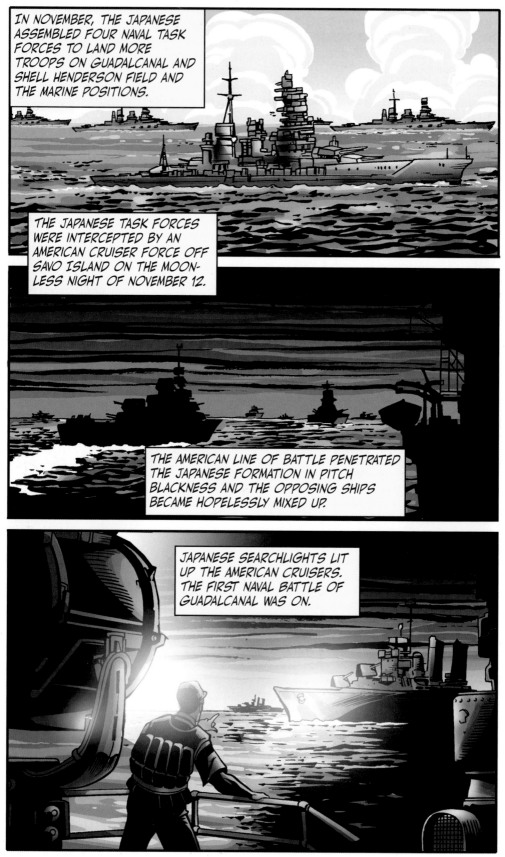

IN NOVEMBER, THE JAPANESE ASSEMBLED FOUR NAVAL TASK FORCES TO LAND MORE TROOPS ON GUADALCANAL AND SHELL HENDERSON FIELD AND THE MARINE POSITIONS.

THE JAPANESE TASK FORCES WERE INTERCEPTED BY AN AMERICAN CRUISER FORCE OFF SAVO ISLAND ON THE MOON-LESS NIGHT OF NOVEMBER 12.

THE AMERICAN LINE OF BATTLE PENETRATED THE JAPANESE FORMATION IN PITCH BLACKNESS AND THE OPPOSING SHIPS BECAME HOPELESSLY MIXED UP.

JAPANESE SEARCHLIGHTS LIT UP THE AMERICAN CRUISERS. THE FIRST NAVAL BATTLE OF GUADALCANAL WAS ON.

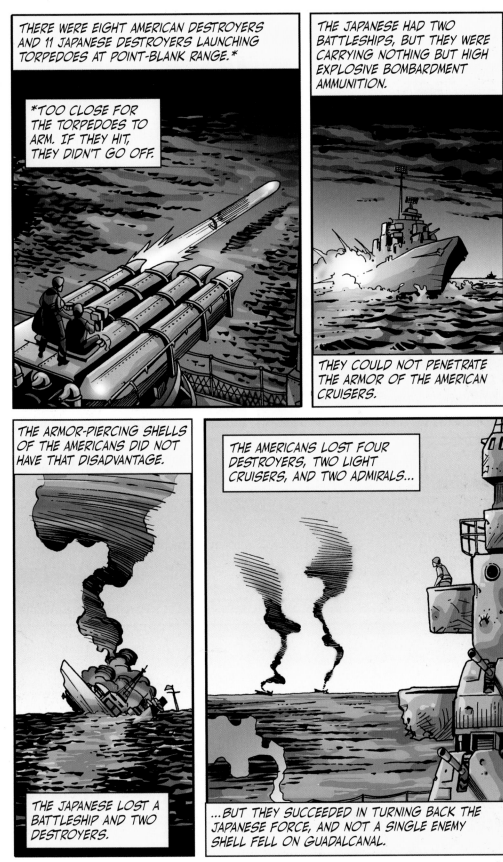

THERE WERE EIGHT AMERICAN DESTROYERS AND 11 JAPANESE DESTROYERS LAUNCHING TORPEDOES AT POINT-BLANK RANGE.*

*TOO CLOSE FOR THE TORPEDOES TO ARM. IF THEY HIT, THEY DIDN'T GO OFF.

THE JAPANESE HAD TWO BATTLESHIPS, BUT THEY WERE CARRYING NOTHING BUT HIGH EXPLOSIVE BOMBARDMENT AMMUNITION.

THEY COULD NOT PENETRATE THE ARMOR OF THE AMERICAN CRUISERS.

THE ARMOR-PIERCING SHELLS OF THE AMERICANS DID NOT HAVE THAT DISADVANTAGE.

THE JAPANESE LOST A BATTLESHIP AND TWO DESTROYERS.

THE AMERICANS LOST FOUR DESTROYERS, TWO LIGHT CRUISERS, AND TWO ADMIRALS...

...BUT THEY SUCCEEDED IN TURNING BACK THE JAPANESE FORCE, AND NOT A SINGLE ENEMY SHELL FELL ON GUADALCANAL.

29

CAPTAIN YOKOTA IN JAPANESE SUBMARINE *I-26* THOUGHT HE HAD THE AMERICAN HEAVY CRUISER *SAN FRANCISCO* IN HIS PERISCOPE SIGHTS.

HE FIRED A SPREAD OF TORPEDOES, BUT ALL OF THEM MISSED THE *SAN FRANCISCO*.

AMERICAN LIGHT CRUISER *JUNEAU*, ALREADY BADLY DAMAGED, TOOK A DIRECT HIT FROM ONE OF YOKOTA'S STRAY TORPEDOES.

MOMENTS LATER, THE *JUNEAU'S* MAGAZINE* EXPLODED AND THE SHIP BLEW APART INTO TWO PIECES.

*WHERE THE SHELLS FOR THE BIG GUNS ARE STORED.

BECAUSE OF THE DANGER FROM SUBMARINES, NO AMERICAN SHIPS STOPPED TO PICK UP SURVIVORS.

IT WAS DAYS BEFORE A RESCUE WAS ATTEMPTED. OUT OF A CREW OF 600, ONLY TEN MEN WERE FOUND ALIVE.

THE FIVE SULLIVAN BROTHERS ALL WENT DOWN WITH THE JUNEAU.

THEY HAD ALL ENLISTED AFTER PEARL HARBOR AND INSISTED ON SERVING ON THE SAME SHIP TOGETHER.

ADMIRAL "BULL" HALSEY, WHO HAD JUST ASSUMED OVERALL COMMAND OF THE PACIFIC FROM ADMIRAL GHORMLEY, WAS FURIOUS.

CAPTAIN YOKOTA SURVIVED THE WAR. WHEN HE RETURNED TO HIS HOMETOWN OF HIROSHIMA, HE FOUND THAT IT NO LONGER EXISTED.*

HALSEY, THE RECIPIENT OF TWO GOLD NAVY LIFESAVING MEDALS, ORDERED THAT ALL EFFORTS WERE TO BE MADE TO PICK UP SURVIVORS.

* DESTROYED BY AN ATOMIC BOMB DROPPED ON AUGUST 6, 1945.

ON NOVEMBER 14, THE JAPANESE SENT ANOTHER TASK FORCE TO ATTACK GUADALCANAL. THIS TIME, AMERICAN BATTLESHIPS WERE THERE TO MEET THEM.

THE U.S. BATTLESHIP *SOUTH DAKOTA* TOOK 47 DIRECT HITS.

CALVIN GRAHAM, A SAILOR ON THE *SOUTH DAKOTA*, SAVED FELLOW CREWMEN DESPITE BEING SERIOUSLY WOUNDED. HE WAS RECOMMENDED FOR THE BRONZE STAR.

WHILE HE WAS RECOVERING FROM HIS WOUNDS, IT WAS DISCOVERED THAT GRAHAM WAS 12 YEARS OLD.

DESPITE HIS BRAVERY, HE WAS DISHONORABLY DISCHARGED FOR LYING ON HIS ENLISTMENT PAPERS, AND ALL HIS MEDALS WERE TAKEN AWAY.

ON GUADALCANAL ISLAND, THE SITUATION FOR THE MARINES BEGAN TO IMPROVE IN NOVEMBER.

THE MARINES ATTACKED THE MATANIKAU REGION OVER BRIDGES ERECTED BY THE 1ST ENGINEER BATTALION.

ELEMENTS OF THE 3RD BATTALION, 5TH MARINES, RAN INTO A STRONG JAPANESE FORCE BETWEEN THE COASTAL ROAD AND THE BEACH.

COMPANY I, OF THE 3RD BATTALION, LED BY CAPTAIN ERSKINE WELLS, ATTACKED WITH FIXED BAYONETS AND ROUTED THE ENEMY.

THIS WAS THE ONLY DOCUMENTED BAYONET CHARGE OF THE CAMPAIGN.

LT. COL. HERMAN H. HANNEKEN LED THE 2ND BATTALION, 7TH MARINES, INTO THE KOLI POINT AREA TO DRIVE OUT THE REMNANTS OF THE ENEMY.

AN AIR STRIKE WAS CALLED IN TO HELP THEM, BUT THE U.S. PLANES BOMBED AND STRAFED THE MARINES BY ACCIDENT.

THEY RAN INTO A JAPANESE BATTALION THAT HAD JUST LANDED THERE.

WITH THE ARRIVAL OF REINFORCEMENTS, THE MARINES ATTACKED AND DROVE THE JAPANESE BACK TO THE BEACH AND SURROUNDED THEM.

VERY FEW, IF ANY, OF THE ENEMY ESCAPED ALIVE.

STARTING ON NOVEMBER 5, LT. COL. EVANS CARLSON LED HIS 2ND MARINE RAIDER BATTALION ON AN EPIC LONG-RANGE PATROL.

THEIR MISSION WAS TO CLEAR OUT THE ENEMY WHO HAD SURVIVED THE MATANIKAU AND KOLI POINT OPERATIONS.

AFTER 30 DAYS, AND 150 MILES OF MARCHING, "CARLSON'S RAIDERS" CAPTURED AND DESTROYED NUMEROUS ARTILLERY PIECES...

...AND KILLED NEARLY 500 ENEMY SOLDIERS.

AT THE END OF NOVEMBER, THE JAPANESE TRIED TO RESUPPLY THEIR TROOPS WITH A DESTROYER TASK FORCE.

IT WAS UNSUCCESSFUL.

IN DECEMBER, THE U.S. ARMY AMERICAL DIVISION ARRIVED AT GUADALCANAL ALONG WITH MASSIVE AMOUNTS OF SUPPLIES AND EQUIPMENT.

THE MARINES WERE PULLED OUT. THEY HAD GONE THROUGH FOUR MONTHS OF CONTINUAL GRUELING COMBAT.

HENDERSON FIELD WAS IMPROVED WITH STEEL MATTING SO IT COULD BE USED IN ALL WEATHER CONDITIONS.

POWERFUL NEW P-38 "LIGHTNING" FIGHTERS, AND B-17 "FLYING FORTRESS" BOMBERS WERE BASED AT THE FIELD.

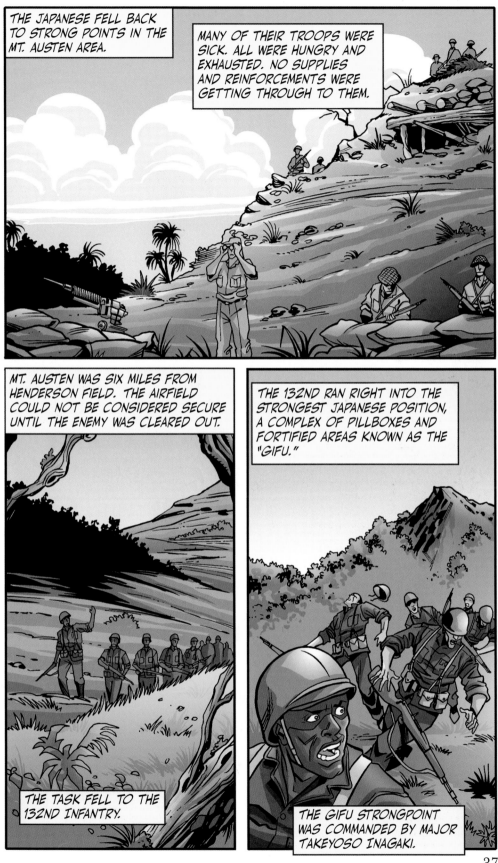

THE JAPANESE FELL BACK TO STRONG POINTS IN THE MT. AUSTEN AREA.

MANY OF THEIR TROOPS WERE SICK. ALL WERE HUNGRY AND EXHAUSTED. NO SUPPLIES AND REINFORCEMENTS WERE GETTING THROUGH TO THEM.

MT. AUSTEN WAS SIX MILES FROM HENDERSON FIELD. THE AIRFIELD COULD NOT BE CONSIDERED SECURE UNTIL THE ENEMY WAS CLEARED OUT.

THE TASK FELL TO THE 132ND INFANTRY.

THE 132ND RAN RIGHT INTO THE STRONGEST JAPANESE POSITION, A COMPLEX OF PILLBOXES AND FORTIFIED AREAS KNOWN AS THE "GIFU."

THE GIFU STRONGPOINT WAS COMMANDED BY MAJOR TAKEYOSO INAGAKI.

THE AMERICAN SOLDIERS HAD TO FIGHT HARD FOR EVERY INCH OF GROUND.

TRAILS HAD TO BE HACKED OUT OF STEEP HILLSIDES. SUPPLIES HAD TO BE CARRIED IN BY HAND.

AFTER 22 DAYS OF CONSTANT INTENSE JUNGLE WARFARE, THE 132ND WAS RELIEVED BY 2ND BATTALION, 35TH INFANTRY.

YOU KNOCK 'EM DEAD, BOYS!

WE SURE AIN'T HERE TO PLAY PATTY-CAKE WITH THEM...

THE ENEMY DEFENDING THE GIFU WERE DESPERATE MEN WHO WERE DETERMINED TO FIGHT TO THE DEATH.

THREE TANKS WERE SENT TO SUPPORT THE G.I.S, BUT ONLY ONE MADE IT TO THE FIGHT.

IT WAS ENOUGH TO BREAK THROUGH INTO THE HEART OF THE GIFU.

MAJOR INAGAKI HAD BEEN ORDERED TO PULL OUT HIS TROOPS, BUT MANY WERE TOO SICK OR WOUNDED TO MARCH.

FACED WITH THE CHOICE OF OBEYING HIS ORDERS OR ABANDONING HIS MEN, HE DECIDED ON A LAST ALL-OUT ATTACK.

AT THIS POINT HE HAD BARELY A HUNDRED MEN CAPABLE OF STANDING AND FIGHTING.

MAJOR INAGAKI AND 85 OF HIS SOLDIERS DIED IN THE ATTACK.

THE REMAINING ENEMY TROOPS FLED FOR THEIR LIVES.

JAPANESE HIGH COMMAND ORDERED GENERAL HYAKUTAKE TO WITHDRAW HIS ENTIRE 17TH ARMY FROM GUADALCANAL.

THE GENERAL TOLD HIS TROOPS THAT THEY WERE BEING PULLED OUT TO TAKE PART IN ANOTHER OPERATION, RATHER THAN ADMIT TO A RETREAT.

THERE WAS INTENSE FIGHTING AS THE JAPANESE FOUGHT A WELL-PLANNED DELAYING ACTION.

THIS ALLOWED THE BULK OF THEIR FORCE TO FALL BACK TO CAPE ESPERANCE, THE NORTHWEST CORNER OF GUADALCANAL.

A CONVOY OF JAPANESE DESTROYERS MADE THREE RESCUE RUNS IN THE FIRST WEEK OF FEBRUARY. ALL OF HYAKUTAKE'S MEN ESCAPED TO FIGHT AGAIN.

BUT THE FIRST PHASE OF THE SOLOMONS CAMPAIGN WAS OVER, AND THE AMERICANS HAD WON IT.

GUADALCANAL PROVED THAT THE JAPANESE WERE NOT UNBEATABLE IN THE PACIFIC. IT ALSO PROVED THE EFFECTIVENESS OF AMPHIBIOUS WARFARE.

GUADALCANAL BECAME ONE OF THE MOST IMPORTANT NAVAL AND AIR BASES IN THE REGION. MANY MAJOR OPERATIONS WERE LAUNCHED FROM THERE.

TOTAL U.S. ARMY AND MARINE LOSSES WERE 1,752 DEAD OR MISSING AND 4,359 WOUNDED.

THE JAPANESE SUFFERED 25,400 DEAD FROM ALL SERVICES.

THE U.S. NAVY LOST 2 CARRIERS, 8 CRUISERS, AND 14 DESTROYERS, AND 4,263 SAILORS.

THE IMPERIAL NAVY LOST 2 BATTLESHIPS, 1 CARRIER, 4 CRUISERS, 12 DESTROYERS, 6 SUBMARINES, AND 1,800 AIRCRAFT WITH THEIR CREWS.

AFTER THE JAPANESE SURRENDER IN 1945, WHEN VICE ADMIRAL TAKEO KURITA WAS ASKED WHAT HE FELT WAS THE TURNING POINT OF THE WAR, HE REPLIED, "GUADALCANAL."

SGT. JOHN BASILONE COULD HAVE SPENT THE REST OF THE WAR SELLING WAR BONDS, BUT HE ASKED TO RETURN TO COMBAT.

HE WAS KILLED IN ACTION ON IWO JIMA IN 1945.

ALBERT SCHMID RECOVERED PARTIAL VISION IN ONE EYE. HE CAME HOME A HERO AND A HOLLYWOOD MOVIE, *PRIDE OF THE MARINES*, WAS MADE ABOUT HIM.

HE GOT MARRIED, MOVED TO FLORIDA, AND SPENT A LOT OF TIME FISHING.

CALVIN GRAHAM SPENT MOST OF THE REST OF HIS LIFE FIGHTING FOR AN HONORABLE DISCHARGE AND THE RETURN OF HIS MEDALS, ESPECIALLY HIS PURPLE HEART.

IT WAS FINALLY PRESENTED TO HIS WIDOW TWO YEARS AFTER HE DIED.

SGT. JACOB VOUZA WAS AWARDED BOTH THE AMERICAN SILVER STAR AND THE BRITISH GEORGE MEDAL FOR HIS VALOR ON GUADALCANAL.

IN 1979 HE WAS KNIGHTED BY QUEEN ELIZABETH II.

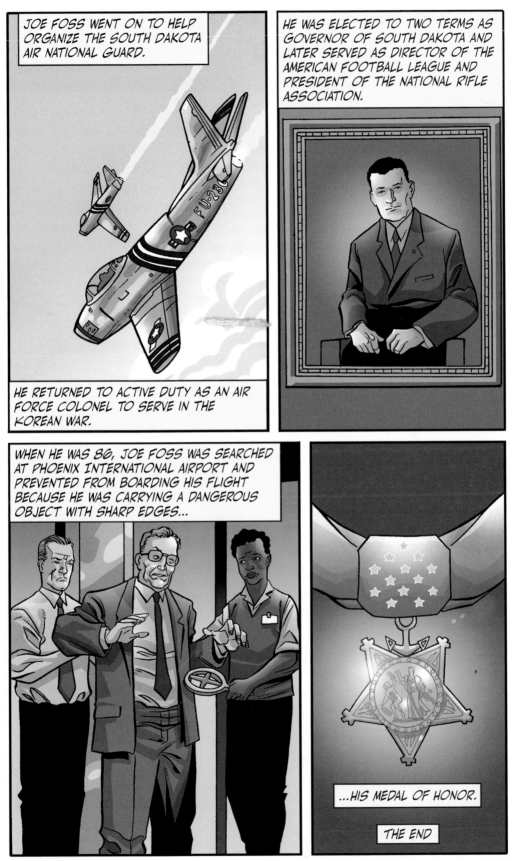

JOE FOSS WENT ON TO HELP ORGANIZE THE SOUTH DAKOTA AIR NATIONAL GUARD.

HE WAS ELECTED TO TWO TERMS AS GOVERNOR OF SOUTH DAKOTA AND LATER SERVED AS DIRECTOR OF THE AMERICAN FOOTBALL LEAGUE AND PRESIDENT OF THE NATIONAL RIFLE ASSOCIATION.

HE RETURNED TO ACTIVE DUTY AS AN AIR FORCE COLONEL TO SERVE IN THE KOREAN WAR.

WHEN HE WAS 86, JOE FOSS WAS SEARCHED AT PHOENIX INTERNATIONAL AIRPORT AND PREVENTED FROM BOARDING HIS FLIGHT BECAUSE HE WAS CARRYING A DANGEROUS OBJECT WITH SHARP EDGES...

...HIS MEDAL OF HONOR.

THE END

Despite the Allied victory at Guadalcanal, the Japanese were far from finished. On November 13, a Japanese battleship group approached Guadalcanal. In the way were two U.S. task forces. In the fighting, the Japanese sunk cruiser *Atlanta* and four destroyers. The Japanese lost two destroyers and the battleship *Hiel*, which was finished off the next day by U.S. planes.

The Japanese came back the next day. Planes from *Enterprise* and Henderson Field caught a Japanese troop convoy. They sank a cruiser and six transports and turned back the rest of the convoy. However, that afternoon, the Japanese submarine *I-26* got the U.S. cruiser *Juneau*–and another Japanese battleship bombardment group was still coming.

Running out of ships, Admiral Halsey sent battleships *South Dakota* and *Washington* to stop the Japanese battleship group. The United States lost three destroyers that night but sank the battleship *Kirishima*, again finished off by planes in the morning. This ended the last Japanese attempt to reinforce the island.

The final naval battle occurred off Tassafaronga on November 30. Again it was a night victory for the Japanese, who sank the cruiser *Northhampton* and badly damaged three others for the loss of one destroyer. But the Japanese mission to resupply the island had failed.

The Tokyo Express made its last resupply attempt on December 11, when a U.S. PT boat sank the Japanese admiral's flagship out from under him. Now it was the Japanese troops ashore on their own.

In December, the 1st Marine Division was at last relieved. One-third were declared medically unfit for duty. The army and a fresh marine regiment took over.

U.S. admiral William Halsey was a forceful commander, with a no-nonsense attitude toward defeating the enemy.

Japanese resistance during the fighting was fierce. Here, U.S. Marines take cover behind their antitank gun and jeep, while others carry off a wounded American soldier.

In December and January they carried out operations against stubborn Japanese remnants around the airfield. The Japanese navy managed to get out many of the survivors in early February.

The Japanese lost two battleships, an aircraft carrier, four cruisers, twelve destroyers, six submarines, and 1,800 aircraft and their crews. Japanese casualties included 25,400 dead, including 9,000 from disease.

The United States lost 6,111 marines and soldiers ashore, including 1,752 dead or missing. At sea, the navy lost two carriers, eight cruisers (including Australian *Canberra*), fourteen destroyers, and 4,263 sailors dead, drowned, or missing in shark-infested seas. Aircraft and aircrew losses were high, but with production and training programs these would be replaced.

Japan could not replace anything.

ammo Short for ammunition; the bullets, shells, grenades, rockets, and bombs that can be exploded or fired from guns or other weapons.

amphibious Launched from the sea against an enemy on land.

antiaircraft Designed for defense against air attack.

artillery Large, heavy guns that are mounted on wheels or tracks.

barrage A heavy outpouring of many things at once.

battalion A large body of soldiers organized as a unit; two or more battalions form a regiment.

battleship A class of warship of the largest size, having the heaviest guns and armor.

convoy A group of ships or motor vehicles traveling together for protection or convenience.

cruiser A medium-sized warship of high speed and a large cruising range, with less armor and firepower than a battleship.

depth charge An explosive device designed for use underwater.

destroyer A small, fast, highly maneuverable warship armed with missiles, guns, torpedoes, and depth charges.

discharge To officially send someone away from a place.

dishonorable discharge To officially be dismissed from the U.S. Army for a serious offense such as sabotage, espionage, lying, cowardice, or murder.

distract To draw someone's attention away from something.

grueling Very tiring; exhausting.

intercept To take, grab, or stop something on its way from one place to another.

pillbox A small concrete structure for a machine gun or other weapon.

reservist A member of a military group who is held back from action for later use.

rout To cause someone to run away from a battle.

salvo A discharge of two or more guns at the same time.

screening duty An arrangement of ships, aircraft, and/or submarines to protect a main body or convoy.

Solomon Islands, or Solomons A nation in Melanesia, east of Papua New Guinea, consisting of nearly one thousand islands. The capital is Honiara, located on the island of Guadalcanal.

strafe To shoot at someone or something from close range, especially with machine gun fire from low-flying aircraft.

torpedo A cylindrical, self-propelled underwater projectile launched from an airplane, a ship, or a submarine and designed to explode against or near a target.

transport A ship, aircraft, or land vehicle designed primarily for carrying personnel and supplies.

FOR MORE INFORMATION

ORGANIZATIONS

National Guadalcanal Memorial Museum
6151 Portage Road
Kalamazoo, MI 49002-3003
(866) 524-7966
Web site: http://www.airzoo.org/

National Museum of the Marine Corps
Quantico, VA 22134
(703) 432-4877
Web site: http://www.usmcmuseum.org/Programs_museum.asp

FOR FURTHER READING

Black, Wallace B., and Jean F. Blashfield. *Guadalcanal*. New York: Macmillan Publishing Company, 1992.

Frank, Richard B. *Guadalcanal: The Definitive Account of the Landmark Battle*. New York: Penguin Books USA, Inc., 1992.

Mueller, Joseph. *Guadalcanal 1942, The Marines Strike Back*. Oxford, England: Osprey Publishing, 1992.

Tregaskis, Richard. *Guadalcanal Diary*. New York: Random House, Inc., 2000.

INDEX

WEB SITES

Due to the changing nature of Internet links, the Rosen Publishing Group, Inc. has developed an online list of Web sites related to the subject of this book. This site is updated regularly. Please use this link to access the list:

http://www.rosenlinks.com/gbww2/guad